MW00852587

"Gator's Out," Said the Trout

Story by Janie Spaht Gill, Ph.D.
Illustrations by Bob Reese

DOMINIE PRESS
Pearson Learning Group

"Gator's out," said the trout.

4

"He's getting near,"
said the deer.

"There's no mistake,"

said the snake.

"I'm scared!" said the bear.

"I think I should scat!"
said the rat.

"Into my house,"
said the mouse.

"Into my hole,"
said the mole.

"We are going to die,"

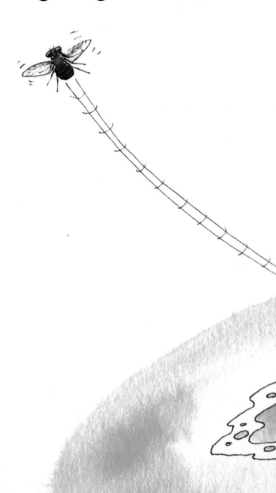

said the fly.

"He will eat us up,"

said the duck.

"Oh, gee," said the flea.
"I wonder why they are
afraid of me."

Curriculum Extension Activities

"Gator's Out," Said the Trout

■ Make a rhyming chart by having the children write and illustrate a word on one sheet of paper, and then write and illustrate a rhyming word on a second sheet of paper. Then have them glue their two pictures next to each other on a chart.

■ Design a swamp scene on a mural, featuring water, trees, lily pads, and grass. Have the children draw their favorite animal in the story and glue it to the swamp scene. Additional swamp animals not mentioned in the story may be added.

■ Give each child a paper plate to design an animal mask for the story. The children may use markers to draw appropriate features and facial expressions. Then they can use their masks to act out the story.

■ Explain the four stages in the life of a fly: egg, larva, pupa, and adult fly. Have the children draw a picture for each stage and write the word for that stage beneath it. Then they could draw pictures of alligators and design a net out of yarn or string. They could add speech bubbles to describe how the alligator feels about being caught.

About the Author

Dr. Janie Spaht Gill brings twenty-five years of teaching experience to her books for young children. During her career thus far, she has taught at every grade level, from kindergarten through college. Gill has a Ph.D. in reading education, with a minor in creative writing. She is currently residing in Lafayette, Louisiana with her husband, Richard. Her fresh, humorous topics are inspired by the things her students say in the classroom. Gill was voted the 1999-2000 Louisiana Elementary Teacher of the Year for her outstanding work in primary education.

Copyright © 2003 by Pearson Education, Inc., publishing as Dominie Press, an imprint of Pearson Learning Group, 299 Jefferson Road, Parsippany, NJ 07054.

All rights reserved. No part of this book may be reproduced or transmitted in any form or by any means, electronic, or mechanical, including photocopying, recording, or by any information storage and retrieval system, without permission in writing from the publisher. For information regarding permission(s), write to Rights and Permissions Department.

Softcover Edition ISBN 0-7685-2154-8
Library Bound Edition ISBN 0-7685-2462-8

Printed in Singapore
  2 3 4 5 6 7 8 9 10   10 09 08 07 06 05

Dominie
Press

Pearson Learning Group

1-800-321-3106
www.pearsonlearning.com